INVADERS
FROM EARTH

INVASIVE
REPTILE AND
AMPHIBIAN
SPECIES

Richard Spilsbury

PowerKiDS
press

New York

Published in 2015 by **The Rosen Publishing Group**
29 East 21st Street, New York, NY 10010

Library of Congress Cataloging-in-Publication Data

Spilsbury, Richard, 1963- author.
 Invasive reptile and amphibian species / Richard Spilsbury.
    pages cm. – (Invaders from Earth)
 Includes bibliographical references and index.
 ISBN 978-1-4994-0068-7 (pbk.)
 ISBN 978-1-4994-0035-9 (6 pack)
 ISBN 978-1-4994-0059-5 (library binding)
 1. Introduced reptiles–Juvenile literature. 2. Introduced amphibians–Juvenile
literature. 3. Biological invasions–Juvenile literature. 4. Environmental disasters–
Juvenile literature. I. Title.
 QL606.S65 2015
 597.916'2–dc23

                                        2014028148

Produced for Rosen by Calcium
Editors for Calcium: Sarah Eason and Robyn Hardyman
Designer: Paul Myerscough

Photo credits: Cover: Shutterstock: Dirk Ercken; Inside: Dreamstime: Andrey Armyagov
23t, Lukas Blazek 19b, David Davis 23b, Foxyjoshi 11t, Péter Gudella 28–29, Attila Jandi
17b, Marek Jelínek 2–3, 22–23, 30–31, 32, Evan Luthye 1, 20b, Dean Pennala 26–27, Lefteris
Papaulakis 20–21, Pixelliste 16–17, Rixie 8–9, S. D. Bower 10b, Luis Lopes Silva 28b, Peter
Vrabel 21b, Anke Van Wyk 18–19, 19t; FLPA: Ingo Arndt/Minden Pictures 18t; Shutterstock:
Alucard2100 17t, 25t, Andi Berger 4b, Dean Bertoncelj 9r, Steve Bower 10–11, Darren J.
Bradley 15b, Brberrys 20t, Cindy Creighton 4–5, Ingrid Curry 14–15, Erni 24b, 24–25, J'nel
12b, 12–13, Cathy Keifer 22b, Heiko Kiera 5t, 6b, 6–7, 7t, 7b, Brian Lasenby 14, Itinerant
Lens 25b, Don Mammoser 26–27, Manja 29t, Nashepard 11b, Reptiles4all 5b, 16, Audrey
Snider-Bell 26t, Aleksey Stemmer 8, Ilias Strachinis 15t, Taboga 27r, G Tipene 9l, Trent
Townsend 13t, WithGod 29b.

Manufactured in the United States of America

CPSIA Compliance Information: Batch CW15PK: For Further Information contact
Rosen Publishing, New York, New York at 1-800-237-9932

CONTENTS

INVADER ALERT

Earth is under attack by **invaders**! These **species** are animals that belong in one area of the world but are moved to another. In these new areas, they harm the plants, animals, or even the humans living there. **Reptiles** and **amphibians** are some of the world's worst invaders.

Getting Around

Some reptiles and amphibians are introduced to new places to control insect pests or as pets. Some escape or are released by owners who can no longer care for them. Others arrive in new places by accident. For example, they may climb into a vehicle and are then carried to a new place.

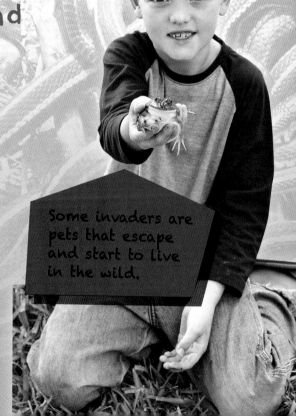

Some invaders are pets that escape and start to live in the wild.

Reptiles hatch from eggs on land. Amphibians hatch from eggs in water. The animals that do best in new places are ones that lay many eggs at one time. This allows their numbers to increase quickly.

SNAKE HATCHING FROM AN EGG

Survival Instinct

Reptiles and amphibians may have few **predators** in the places they invade. They may be bigger or more aggressive than local species, so they take a larger share of any available food.

AGGRESSIVE SNAKE

5

BURMESE PYTHON

Burmese pythons are the biggest reptiles to attack the United States. These snakes are native to Southeast Asia. They spread to the United States as pets. Some were released into the wild in Florida by their owners. Others escaped after Hurricane Andrew damaged pet stores in 1992.

BURMESE PYTHON

A Deadly Embrace

Burmese pythons are dangerous predators. They hunt at night and kill their **prey** by coiling their bodies around it and squeezing it to death. In the Florida **wetlands** the snakes feed on more than 20 different types of animals, including **mammals**, birds, and reptiles.

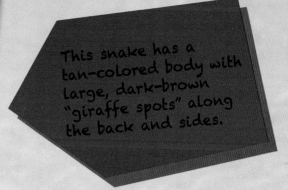

This snake has a tan-colored body with large, dark-brown "giraffe spots" along the back and sides.

Under Threat

Burmese pythons can kill prey as big as the huge American alligators that live in the Everglades. They also kill **endangered** species such as wood storks and Key Largo rats. Even Florida panthers could be at risk.

PYTHON EGGS

INVADER ANALYSIS

Burmese pythons grow to more than 20 feet (6 m) long. They live for up to 25 years. Females start breeding from the age of 4 and lay up to 100 eggs each year. These snakes can quickly increase their numbers.

CANE TOAD

Cane toads are native to South and Central America. They were introduced into Australia on purpose in the 1930s to feed on beetles that were damaging sugarcane plants. The toads ate many small animals but not the insects they were brought in to kill.

Terrible Toads

Cane toads eat many kinds of small animals, such as snails, bees, and other insects. This is causing the number of these animals to fall. It also affects other amphibians, because there are fewer small animals for them to eat. Their numbers then decrease, too.

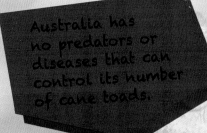

Australia has no predators or diseases that can control its number of cane toads.

Poisoned

Adult cane toads produce poison through their skin when they are attacked. This means that most of their predators, such as dingoes, crocodiles, kookaburras, and lizards, die soon after eating them.

In the 1930s, just over 100 cane toads were introduced to Australia. Now there are more than 1.5 billion of them. They have spread over an area bigger than the states of Texas and Oklahoma combined.

KOOKABURRA

FRILL-NECKED LIZARD

CUBAN TREE FROG

Cuban tree frogs are native to Cuba, the Cayman Islands, and the Bahamas. They were accidentally brought to Florida during the 1920s in containers on cargo ships.

Night Hunter

This tree frog hunts small animals at night. It eats almost any prey it can find, including lizards, insects, spiders, and small snakes. When it swallows its prey, its big, bulging eyeballs sink into its head. They help to push the frog's meal down its throat.

Cuban tree frogs release a substance that irritates skin, so people should not touch them.

Cuban tree frogs move into people's homes, where they lurk near lights to catch insects to eat. They stain walls with their droppings. They sometimes get into bathrooms and clog sink drains. They even invade power boxes and cause power outages.

CUBAN TREE FROG ON A WINDOW FRAME

Frogs in Danger

Cuban tree frogs eat at least five different species of **native** tree frog. They also compete with these frogs for food. Their tadpoles compete with native tadpoles for space and food, too. All this is causing populations of native tree frogs to decline.

TADPOLES

BROWN TREE SNAKE

Brown tree snakes come from Australia and Indonesia. When they invaded the island of Guam in the Pacific Ocean they caused the **extinction** of several native bird, reptile, bat, and amphibian species.

GUAM

Accidental Arrivals

These snakes arrived in Guam by accident when a few of them slithered into military aircraft and cargo ships after World War II. On Guam the snakes had no predators or competitors and the birds there were easy to catch, so the snakes' numbers grew quickly.

Deadly Bites

Brown tree snakes have **venomous** bites that kill quickly. They can climb fast and high, and they can jump across huge gaps between trees. They have killed off 10 of Guam's 11 native forest bird species. The snakes regularly cause power outages by crawling on power lines.

This greedy snake hunts many animals: birds, rodents, lizards, and even small mammals.

INVADER ANALYSIS

Only a **few** brown tree snakes arrived in Guam in the 1950s, but now the forests are **full of them**. Today, there are 2 million of them on an island that is only **30 miles (50 km)** long and 6 **miles (10 km) wide**.

BULLFROG

One reason bullfrogs are a problem invader is that they spread so fast. They spread quickly because the young frogs are on the run from adult bullfrogs that try to eat them!

Cannibal Frogs

Bullfrogs eat almost anything that fits in their big mouths: birds, rats, snakes, lizards, turtles, fish, other frogs, and each other. Adult bullfrogs eat young bullfrogs, so the young frogs escape to new ponds. They can travel about 6 miles (almost 10 km) in a few weeks.

A bullfrog can measure 8 inches (20 cm) long, leap up to 3 feet (1 m), and live for nearly 10 years.

EARTH UNDER ATTACK

Bullfrogs are native to eastern North America. They were transported around the world for use as food. They are now established in at least 15 countries, as well as in western North America.

BULLFROG

TADPOLE

Bullfrog Bullies

Bullfrogs soon take over a new pond because females lay about 20,000 eggs at one time. The frogs that hatch compete with native amphibians for food and eat many native frogs. Bullfrogs have caused a decline in native amphibian and reptile species in much of North America.

TEGU LIZARD

Tegu lizards are originally from South America, but these giant reptiles are invading the United States. They have been seen in Florida where experts think they were once kept as pets. They escaped, or were released, into the wild when they grew too big to be kept.

Tegu Talent

Tegu lizards can swim, but they live mostly on land where they eat a wide variety of foods. These include fruits, vegetables, insects, and small animals. They survive the winter months in Florida by **hibernating** in burrows that they dig or steal from other animals.

The tegu flicks its tongue to detect the smell of prey.

Egg Eater

One problem with these giant lizards is that they eat the eggs of endangered native species, such as gopher tortoises and American crocodiles. They can also climb shrubs to eat the eggs in the nests of a scrub jay that is found only in Florida.

FIERCE PREDATOR

TEGU LIZARD

INVADER ANALYSIS

Tegu lizards are big, fierce predators. They can weigh more than 30 pounds (13.5 kg). They can grow up to 4 feet (1.2 m) long and have sharp teeth, powerful jaws, and sharp claws.

AFRICAN CLAWED FROG

The African clawed frog is the only amphibian to have claws. It uses the three short claws on its back feet to tear apart its food.

CLAWS

Into the Wild

The African clawed frog is native to southern Africa. It was introduced around the world in the 1940s, when scientists used the frog in tests. After better tests were developed, many frogs were released into the wild. Clawed frogs breed all year round. Their populations grew fast because females lay hundreds of eggs, which grow into adults within 1 year.

EARTH UNDER ATTACK

This frog is hard to stop. It lives for up to 15 years and can even survive when ponds dry up. It burrows into the pond mud, leaving a tunnel to the surface so that it can breathe air. The frog lives in the burrow for up to 1 year. It can also swim or crawl long distances to new ponds.

Fearsome Frog

The African clawed frog is an aggressive predator that eats almost anything it finds. In California, it threatens the survival of animals such as the three-spine stickleback and the red-legged frog. In some US states it is such a pest that it is illegal to own, transport, or sell the frog.

The frog spends most of its time underwater and surfaces only to breathe.

RED-EARED SLIDER

RED-EARED SLIDERS

Red-eared sliders are a kind of turtle native to the southern United States. They have spread throughout North America and many other parts of the world, including Australia, Southeast Asia, South Africa, and parts of Europe.

Survivors

The main reason the turtles are so widespread is that they are sold as cheap aquarium pets. When owners dump them in local lakes and rivers, the turtles breed. They survive because they eat many foods, and in cold winters, they hibernate.

SLIDER SURVIVOR

Taking Over

Red-eared sliders eat plants and animals such as insects, fish, frogs, and birds. They are bigger and more aggressive than native freshwater turtles and compete with them for space and food. They also carry diseases that harm smaller, native turtles but do not affect the red-eared sliders.

INVADER ANALYSIS

Red-eared sliders can **be up** to 12 inches (30 cm) long. **The females lay more eggs** than the native female turtles, which results in even more adult red-eared sliders to take **up** space and food.

These turtles are aggressive and will bite!

VEILED CHAMELEON

A veiled chameleon can lie still for a long time, waiting for an insect to pass by. Then the chameleon shoots out its tongue, catching the prey on the sticky tip, before pulling it quickly back into its mouth.

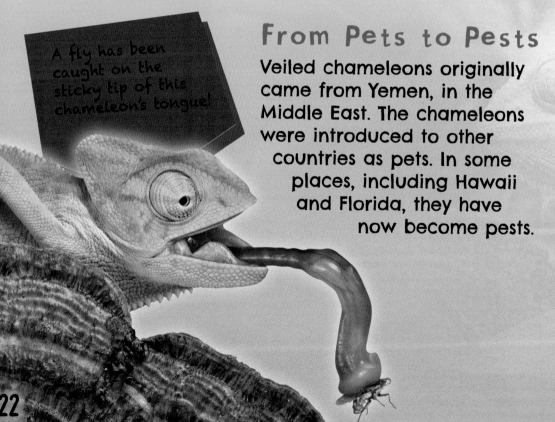

A fly has been caught on the sticky tip of this chameleon's tongue!

From Pets to Pests

Veiled chameleons originally came from Yemen, in the Middle East. The chameleons were introduced to other countries as pets. In some places, including Hawaii and Florida, they have now become pests.

A Threat

Veiled chameleons cause problems because females lay up to 200 eggs each year, so their numbers increase quickly. They eat mainly insects, flowers, and leaves. The chameleons grow up to 2 feet (60 cm) long, and because they are so big, they also catch birds and other small animals.

HARD TO SPOT

VEILED CHAMELEON

EARTH UNDER ATTACK

Veiled chameleons affect a large number of species because they can live in a variety of **habitats**, from dry, flat areas to high, wet mountain regions. They can also live for up to 8 years.

23

SPECTACLED CAIMAN

The spectacled caiman gets its name from the ridge between its eyes which looks like the bridge of a pair of spectacles, or glasses. Its other name is the common caiman. It is the most common type of crocodilian on Earth.

Caimans live in warm, wet places, such as rivers, lakes, and reservoirs.

EARTH UNDER ATTACK

One reason spectacled caimans have spread is that people like to eat beef burgers. In Venezuela, for example, people cleared forest to make space to rear cattle for beef. They made big ponds to collect water for cattle to drink, and caimans came to live in them.

CAIMAN IN THE WATER

Commonest Caiman

Spectacled caimans are native to central and South America. They have spread to parts of North America, including Florida. There they were introduced into the wild when pets escaped or were released because they grew too big.

Supreme Survivor

Caimans survive because they eat any type of food, from insects to deer. Another reason for the success of spectacled caimans is that crocodilian hunters do not want their tough hides. The skins of other types of crocodilian are more valuable.

SPECTACLED CAIMAN

TOKAY GECKO

Tokay geckos often hiss to call to other geckos, but males that want to breed call "to-kay." This is how the gecko got its name.

TOKAY TOES

Great Climber

Tokay geckos can climb glass and smooth walls and can cling to ceilings. The skin on the underside of their toes is covered with tiny hairs that help them cling to most surfaces. The geckos use their climbing skills in homes, to catch insects that gather on windows or near electric lights.

If a predator catches a tokay gecko by its tail, the tail detatches from the body so that the lizard can escape. It then grows a new tail.

26

Pit Bull Lizard

Geckos have a powerful bite. They use it to eat bird eggs in forest nests. They sometimes eat the young of rare birds. Tokay geckos also attack and bite other lizards to keep them away from food sources. They even clamp onto people's fingers if they get too close!

TOKAY GECKO

INVADER ANALYSIS

Tokay geckos are native to Asian countries, including Indonesia and the Philippines. They invaded the Caribbean and some US states, including Hawaii, after pet geckos escaped into the wild.

DEALING WITH INVADERS

The problem of invader reptiles and amphibians may get worse. These animals prefer warm places, and because of the general rise in Earth's temperature, or global warming, they may spread to more new places.

Prevention

Governments are doing all they can to stop new invaders. In many places, they make laws to stop people selling exotic pets or fine people who release their pets into the wild. At ports and airports, officials use sniffer dogs to check if animals are inside cargo.

SNIFFER DOG

BROWN ANOLE

In many parts of Florida, brown anoles eat native green anoles. So far, they have not spread widely because they are less tolerant of cold than green anoles. However, this could change if other areas of the United States get warmer.

Cure

People are also looking for ways to get rid of the animals that have already invaded. They capture some animals and move them back to their original homes. In Guam, people killed some brown tree snakes with poisoned mice. They fitted the mice with parachutes and dropped them from helicopters onto the ground, where the snakes ate them!

AIRPORT CHECKS

GLOSSARY

amphibians Animals that can live both on land and in water, such as frogs.

breeding Producing young or babies.

endangered In danger of dying out completely.

extinction The dying out of a plant or animal.

habitats Places where animals and plants live.

hibernating Passing the winter in a sleeplike state.

invader Something that spreads quickly and causes harm.

mammals Animals that have some hair on their bodies and give birth to live young.

native Born in or belonging to a place.

predators Animals that hunt and eat other animals.

prey An animal that is hunted and eaten by other animals.

reptiles Animals that lay eggs, have scaly or hard skin, and are cold-blooded.

species Types of living things.

venomous Containing venom, or poison.

wetlands Lands that are always wet.

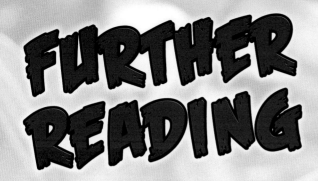

FURTHER READING

Books

Alien Invasion (Current Science). Des Moines, IA: National Geographic Children's Books, 2010.

Cheung, Lisa. *The 10 Most Destructive Ecosystem Invaders* (The 10). London, UK: Franklin Watts, 2010.

Collard III, Sneed B. *Science Warriors Battle Against Invasive Species* (Scientists in the Field). Boston, MA: Houghton Mifflin, 2008.

Websites

Due to the changing nature of Internet links, PowerKids Press has developed an online list of websites related to the subject of this book. This site is updated regularly. Please use this link to access the list:
www.powerkidslinks.com/ife/repamp

INDEX